Storytellers

and Other

Figurative Pottery

Douglas Congdon-Martin

Schiffer Publishing Ltd

77 Lower Valley Road, Atglen, PA 19310

Dandova, Juan. Taos, Nativity (6 piece), 11.5".
Courtesy of Keams Canyon Trading Post.

Printed in China.
ISBN: 0-88740-270-4

Published by Schiffer Publishing, Ltd.
77 Lower Valley Road
Atglen, PA 19310
Please write for a free catalog.
This book may be purchased from the publisher.
Please include $2.95 postage.
Try your bookstore first.

We are interested in hearing from authors
with book ideas on related subjects.

Dedication

To Beth, Josh, Sarah and Liddy.
They people the stories of my life.

Contents

Quintana, Margaret. Cochiti, Female (3 children). *Courtesy of Wind River Trading Company.*

Gratitude

Many people have welcomed us into their shops and homes as we gathered information and photographs for this book. We thank them all for their contribution. You will find their names listed below, and we have included the addresses of those with businesses where you will find storytellers for sale. Credits are given with each of the photographs.

Some people need special recognition. Caroline and Joseph Gachupin showed us warm hospitality. With all of our equipment they welcomed us into their home, where we photographed them while they crafted storytellers. They introduced us to their family and to the taste of Jemez cuisine. Marvelous!

Special thanks also goes to Alexander E. Anthony and his team at Adobe Gallery. Al is the midwife of the storytellers and figurines, having given it a showcase and exposure in his gallery. He also shared his first hand knowledge of the development of the storyteller, allowed us to photograph in his gallery, and shared his exhaustive photo archives with us. We are grateful.

Eric and Ailene Bromberg encouraged this project and provided the necessary inspiration.

Guy Berger and Steve DePriest at the Palms Trading Company, also permitted us to invade their store and unwrap hundreds of storytellers for photography. They then rewrapped and repriced each of them, a mammoth task. In addition they shared their knowledge of the craft and the artists with us.

Finally, most of the fine photos were taken by Herbert and Peter Schiffer. I thank them for capturing the beauty of these figures on film.

Our sincere thanks go to the following: Adobe Gallery, Alexander Anthony, 413 Romero NW, Albuquerque, New Mexico; Andrews Pueblo Pottery and Art Gallery, Bob, Helen, and Cathy Andrews, 400 San Felipe NW, Albuquerque, New Mexico; Bing Crosby's Indian Art, Inc., Bing Crosby, 2510 Washington NE, Albuquerque, New Mexico; Dewey Galleries, Ltd., Ray Dewey and Peter Waidler, 74 E. San Francisco St., Santa Fe, New Mexico; Foutz Trading Company, Bill and Kay Foutz, Shiprock, New Mexico

Indian Trader West, Tommy Elkins, Willa, Tom, and Brett Bastien, 204 W. San Francisco St., Santa Fe, New Mexico; The Indian Post, Sovereign Building, 609 Hamilton Mall, Allentown, Pennsylvania; McGee & Sons, Keams Canyon Arts and Crafts, Bruce and Ron McGee, Keams Canyon, Arizona; The Kiva Trading Post, Sylvia Leakey and the team, 57 Old Santa Fe Trail, Santa Fe, New Mexico; Palms Trading Company, Guy Berger and Steve DePriest, 1504 Lomas NW, Albuquerque, New Mexico; Rainbow Man, Bob and Marianne Kapoun, 107 E. Palace, Santa Fe, New Mexico; Shiprock Trading Post, Ed and Jeff Foutz, Shiprock, New Mexico Jim Silva, Bernallilo, New Mexico; Turquoise Lady, Mary and Cathren Harris, 2012 Plaza Drive, SW, Albuquerque, New Mexico; Wind River Trading Company, 113 E. San Francisco Street, Santa Fe, New Mexico; Armand and Barbara Winfield.

Cheyenne Jim. Taos, Female (3 children), 8". *Courtesy of Keams Canyon Trading Post.*

Introduction

Even a cursory glance through these pages should be enough to make clear to the reader why storytellers have so captivated collectors and admirers of American Indian art. Each artist brings his or her unique talent to the creation of the figure, and each storyteller has a personality of its own. It is no surprise that demand for these creations continues to rise year after year.

The inventor of the form is Helen Cordero of the Cochiti Pueblo, New Mexico, though the tradition of figurative pottery predates Helen by many centuries. In their excellent book, *The Pueblo Storyteller*, Barbara Babcock, and Guy and Doris Monthan date figurative pottery in the Southwest to perhaps as early 300 B.C. and certainly as early as 400 A.D. among the Anasazi, the predecessors of today's Pueblo Indians.

Discouraged and repressed as idolatrous by European clergy seeking to convert the native Americans, figurative pottery from the period of colonialism is rare, nearly to the point of non-existence. Babcock and the Monthans propose, however, that the tradition of figurative pottery survived, albeit as part of an underground "pattern of secrecy" maintained in the pueblos. It reemerges late in the nineteenth century, spurred on by the arrival by railroad of tourists to the Southwest. They were anxious to purchase examples of Indian art, and the potters were more than willing to oblige.

Much of this tourist pottery manufacturing centered in the Cochiti pueblo. According to Alexander E. Anthony, the potters of Cochiti produced figurines in the likenesses of padres, cowboys, businessmen, and tourists for eager collectors. If the tourists recognized that they were being lampooned by this pottery, it did not seem to quell their enthusiasm.

It was into this potting tradition that Helen Cordero was born in 1915. In the 1950s she was making "Singing Mother" figures. These were sitting female figures holding one or two children on their laps. They were quite popular and were made by many Cochiti potters. In 1964, Helen

Romero, Marie. Cochiti, Female (9 children). *Courtesy of Adobe Gallery.*

Cordero made the innovation which would prove to be a milestone in figurative pottery. Instead of the traditional female figure, she modelled one after her grandfather, Santiago Quintana. The grandfather storyteller, his mouth open and five children clinging to him, was an endearing figure and the public sought more.

We have learned that Helen Cordero believes that the true storyteller is a male figure, and that female figures are properly called "Singing Mothers." As their creator she certainly is an authority on the subject of storytellers, but the form she began has taken on a life of its own. More and more people are making storytellers, at Cochiti, the surrounding pueblos, and even from other peoples like the Navajo, Blackfoot, and Hispanic whose examples are shown in this volume. The term "storyteller" has become generic and is used to describe not only male figures, but females, clowns, mudheads, frogs, owls, turtles, coyotes ...nearly any figure that has an adult figure surrounded by or covered with children.

Alexander Anthony was one of the first

Arquero, Josephine. Cochiti, Figures. *Courtesy of Adobe Gallery.*

Cochiti, goat figure, c. 1900-1920. Red and black glaze on tan clay. Museum of New Mexico artifact #12174/12. Photo by Arthur Taylor. *Courtesy of Adobe Gallery.*

people to recognize the importance of storytellers as an art form. The showings at his Adobe Gallery trace their rise in popularity. The first of these exhibits was in 1979, when storytellers were made by only a handful of artists and known to only a few people. Thirteen storytellers were shown at that first exhibit.

By Mother's Day, 1980, when the second exhibit was held, there were many more storytellers made by thirteen artists. In the flyer for the fourth annual storyteller figurine exhibit in 1982, a minimum of 200 pieces of figurative pottery were anticipated, made by 50 different potters from eleven pueblos. After five years Adobe Gallery had to discontinue the exhibits because they had grown beyond the confines of the gallery.

Interest in storytellers continues to grow. The collectors come from all over the world. Some are looking to own a pot from every artist, while others are looking for only the top of the line, noting how prices have appreciated over the years for the work of Helen Cordero and other early storyteller makers. Many collectors enter the field at a level they can afford, and as their interest and resources grow they upgrade their collections. *Storytellers and Other Figurative Pottery* is designed to be helpful to collectors. The pieces are arranged by pueblo, which are in turn arranged by language groups, following the lead of Babcock, Monthan, and Monthan. Within the pueblos the storytellers are organized alphabetically by the names of the artists. A full alphabetical index is provided at the end of the book.

We hope you will enjoy the volume, and that these wonderful creations may share their stories with you.

Teller, Stella. Isleta, Bear (3 cubs). *Courtesy of Adobe Gallery.*

Maker unknown. Cochiti, Clowns, c. 1950s, 10.25". *Courtesy of Adobe Gallery.*

Arquero, Josephine. Cochiti, Female storyteller (3 children). *Courtesy of Adobe Gallery.*

Arquero, Martha. Cochiti, Female storyteller (5 children), 5". *Courtesy of Palms Trading Company.*

Arquero, Dominic. Cochiti, Females, 1982. *Courtesy of Adobe Gallery.*

Arquero, Martha. Cochiti; Frog (7 froglets), 4.75". *Courtesy of Andrews Pueblo Gallery.*

Arquero, Martha. Cochiti, Bears (4 cubs), 5.5". *Courtesy of Palms Trading Company.*

Brown, Rose M. Cochiti, Male storyteller (21 children), 7.5". *Courtesy of Adobe Gallery.*

8

Chalan, Mary O. Cochiti, Female storyteller (4 children). *Courtesy of Wind River Trading Company.*

Chalan, Mary O. Cochiti, Turtle (3 children), 3.75". *Courtesy of Indian Traders West.*

Chalan, Mary O. Cochiti, Male storyteller (8 children), 11". *Courtesy of Indian Traders West.*

Cordero, Damacia. Cochiti, Female storyteller (2 children), 1980. *Courtesy of Adobe Gallery.*

Cordero, Helen. Cochiti, Male storyteller (9 children), 1970-75. *Courtesy of Dewey Galleries.*

Cordero, Helen. Side view of above photo.

Cordero, George. Cochiti, Turtle (4 children), 5". *Courtesy of The Kiva.*

Cordero, Helen. Cochiti, Male storyteller (7 children), 1989, 9.5". *Courtesy of Jim Silva.*

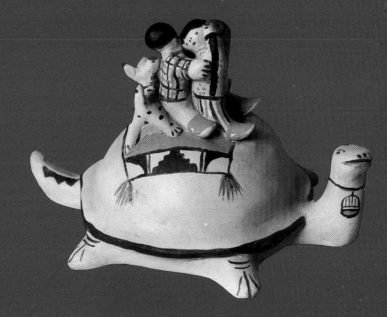

Cordero, Helen. Cochiti, Turtle (2 children). *Courtesy of Adobe Gallery.*

Cordero, Helen. Side view of above photo.

Cordero, Helen. Opposite view of above photo.

Cordero, Helen. Cochiti, Male storyteller (4 children), 1977, 12.5". *Courtesy of Adobe Gallery.*

Cordero, Helen. Cochiti, Male storyteller (8 children), 1990. Helen Cordero's recent work. *Courtesy of Adobe Gallery.*

Eustace, Felicita. Cochiti, Female storyteller (12 children), 7.25". *Courtesy of The Kiva.*

Eustace, Felicita. Cochiti, Mocassin (5 children), 2.5". *Courtesy of Adobe Gallery.*

Herrara, Mary F. . Cochiti, Female storyteller (3 children), 1981, 1.75". *Courtesy of Adobe Gallery (photo: William L. Rada).*

Herrera, Dorothy. Cochiti, Bears, l: 5"; r: 6". *Courtesy of Bing Crosby's.*

Herrera, Dorothy. Cochiti, Frog (3 froglets, 1 lizard), 4.25". *Courtesy of The Kiva.*

Herrera, Dorothy. Cochiti, Polar bear (1 cub), 4". *Courtesy of Andrews Pueblo Gallery.*

Herrera, Dorothy. Cochiti, Storytellers, 6". *Courtesy of Indian Traders West.*

Herrera, Dorothy. Cochiti, Bears (l: 3 cubs; r: 2 cubs), 4.5". *Courtesy of Bing Crosby's.*

Herrera, Dorothy. Cochiti, Bear (5 cubs), 7". *Courtesy of Indian Traders West.*

Herrera, Dorothy. Cochiti, Bears, l-r: 5.5", 4", 5". *Courtesy of Bing Crosby's.*

Herrera, Edwin. Cochiti, Bears, l: 7.625": r: 5.625". *Courtesy of Andrews Pueblo Gallery.*

Herrera, Edwin. Cochiti, Bear, 7.75". *Courtesy of Bing Crosby's.*

Herrera, Edwin. Cochiti, Bear (2 cubs), 5". *Courtesy of Indian Traders West.*

Herrera, Edwin. Cochiti, Nativity (10 pieces), 3.25". *Courtesy of The Kiva.*

16

Hu-u-ca. Cochiti, Clown, 4.5". *Courtesy of Brett Bastien.*

Ke'Shra & H., M.B. Cochiti, Female storyteller (2 children), 1989. *Courtesy of Palms Trading Company.*

Laweka, Marie. Cochiti, Animal figures. *Courtesy of Andrews Pueblo Gallery.*

Laweka, Maria. Cochiti, Female storyteller (2 children), 5.75". *Courtesy of Andrews Pueblo Gallery.*

Lewis, Ivan and Rita. Cochiti, Male storyteller (11 children), 1986. *Courtesy of Adobe Gallery.*

Lewis, Ivan and Rita. Cochiti, Mermaid, 1986. *Courtesy of Adobe Gallery.*

Lewis, Ivan and Rita. Cochiti, Deer, 1986. *Courtesy of Adobe Gallery.*

Lewis, Ivan & Rita. Cochiti, Drummer (4 children), 5.5". *Courtesy of Adobe Gallery.*

Lewis, Ivan and Rita. Cochiti, Male story-teller (3 children), 1986. *Courtesy of Adobe Gallery.*

Lewis, Ivan. Cochiti, Pig, 6" (h) x 13" (l). *Courtesy of Adobe Gallery.*

Lewis, Rita. Cochiti, Nativity (6 pieces), 5.25". *Courtesy of The Kiva.*

Loretto, J.M. Cochiti, Figure, 1989, 4.5". *Courtesy of Palms Trading Company*

Lewis, M. Cochiti, Male storyteller (1 child) , 3.25". *Courtesy of Andrews Pueblo Gallery.*

Lewis, Marie. Cochiti, Female storyteller (3 children), 5". *Courtesy of Andrews Pueblo Gallery.*

Lujan, J. & T. Cochiti, Female storyteller (11 children), 9.25". *Courtesy of Palms Trading Company.*

Martin, Mary. Cochiti, Male storyteller (7 children), 7.5". *Courtesy of Adobe Gallery.*

Martin, Mary. Cochiti, Female storyteller (3 children), 1983. *Courtesy of Adobe Gallery.*

Martin, Mary. Cochiti, Male, 1986. *Courtesy of Adobe Gallery.*

Martin, Mary. Cochiti, Drummer, 1982, 8.25". *Courtesy of Adobe Gallery.*

Naranjo, Louis. Cochiti, Santa (2 children), 7.5″. *Courtesy of Rainbow Man.*

Naranjo, Louis. Cochiti, Priest figure, (9.5″). *Courtesy of Adobe Gallery.*

Naranjo, Louis. Cochiti, Bear (6 cubs), 1986. *Courtesy of Adobe Gallery.*

Naranjo, Louis. Cochiti, Bear (16 cubs), 1986. *Courtesy of Adobe Gallery.*

Naranjo, Louis. Cochiti, Bear (4 cubs), 5". *Courtesy of The Kiva.*

Narango, Louis. Cochiti, Dancing figures and mother with child. *Courtesy of Adobe Gallery.*

Naranjo, Louis. Cochiti, Bears and Foxes, 1986. *Courtesy of Adobe Gallery.*

Naranjo, Louis. Cochiti, Bear (1 cub), 1984. *Courtesy of Adobe Gallery.*

Naranjo, Louis. Cochiti, Fox (3 pups), 1986. *Courtesy of Adobe Gallery.*

23

Nez, P. Cochiti, Female storyteller (5 children),
4". *Courtesy of Palms Trading Company.*

Ortiz, I. Cochiti, Female storyteller (6 children),
3.75". *Courtesy of Palms Trading Company.*

Ortiz, I. Cochiti, Female storyteller (3 children),
3.5". *Courtesy of Palms Trading Company.*

Ortiz, Inez. Cochiti, Children in mocassin, 3.8".
Courtesy of Andrews Pueblo Gallery.

Ortiz, Inez. Cochiti,
Nativity (10 piece).
*Courtesy of Palms
Trading Company.*

Ortiz, Inez. Cochiti, Turtle (2 children). *Courtesy of Adobe Gallery.*

Ortiz, Inez. Cochiti, Three children on drum, 4.75". *Courtesy of Palms Trading Company.*

Ortiz, Inez. Cochiti, Family Groups, 2.75". *Courtesy of Palms Trading Company.*

Ortiz, Inez. Cochiti, Bears, 4". *Courtesy of Palms Trading Company.*

Ortiz, Peferius. Cochiti, Frog (7 froglets), 5". *Courtesy of a private collection.*

Pecos, Monica. Cochiti, Female storyteller (6 children), 6". *Courtesy of Jim Silva.*

Ortiz, Seferina. Cochiti, Drummer, (9.5). *Courtesy of Adobe Gallery.*

Pino, C. Cochiti, Bear figures, 1989, 2.25". *Courtesy of The Kiva.*

Quintana, Mary E. Cochiti, Female storyteller (2 children), 4.5". *Courtesy of Palms Trading Company.*

Quintana, Margaret. Cochiti, Female story-teller (14 children), 17.75". *Courtesy of Wind River Trading Company.*

Quintana, Mary E. Cochiti, Female storyteller (6 children), 6". *Courtesy of Palms Trading Company.*

Quintana, Mary E. Cochiti, Male storyteller (4 children), 5.5". *Courtesy of Palms Trading Company.*

Quintana, Pablo. Cochiti, Females (3 children), 1989, 9.75". *Courtesy of Palms Trading Company.*

Romero, Maria Priscilla. Cochiti, Male story-teller (27 children), 1986. *Courtesy of Adobe Gallery.*

Quintana. Cochiti, Females, l: 3"; r: .75". *Courtesy of Foutz Trading Company.*

Romero, Marie. Cochiti, Female storyteller (6 children), 6.75". *Courtesy of Adobe Gallery.*

Snow Flake Flower (Stephanie C. Rhoades). Cochiti, Nativity (9 piece), 1986. *Courtesy of Andrews Pueblo Gallery.*

Snow Flake Flower (Stephanie C. Rhoades). Cochiti, "Pueblo Woman" (3 children), 1987, 7". *Courtesy of Indian Traders West.*

Snow Flake Flower (Stephanie C. Rhoades). Cochiti, l: "Drummer Boy"; r: "Prayer Offering of a New Born", 1987, l: 7.5"; r: 8.875". *Courtesy of Indian Traders West.*

Suina, Ada. Cochiti, Female storyteller (2 children), 1981. *Courtesy of Adobe Gallery.*

Suina, Ada. Cochiti, Female storyteller (6 children), 8.5". *Courtesy of Palms Trading Company.*

Suina, Ada. Cochiti, Male storyteller (4 children), 6.5". *Courtesy of Andrews Pueblo Gallery.*

Suina, Ada. Cochiti, Female storyteller (4 children), 1988. *Courtesy of Adobe Gallery.*

Suina, Ada. Cochiti, Male storyteller (16 children), 1982. *Courtesy of Adobe Gallery.*

Suina, Ada. Cochiti, Drummer. *Courtesy of Adobe Gallery.*

Suina, Ada. Cochiti, Female storyteller (8 children). *Courtesy of Adobe Gallery.*

Suina, B. Cochiti, Male storyteller (6 children), 9". *Courtesy of Palms Trading Company.*

Suina, Antonita Cordera. Cochiti, Male storyteller (4 children), 7.5". *Courtesy of Adobe Gallery.*

Suina, B. Cochiti, Mudhead (4 children), 7". *Courtesy of Palms Trading Company.*

Suina, B. Cochiti, Female, 6". *Courtesy of Bing Crosby's.*

Suina, Buffy Cordero. Cochiti, Male storyteller (6 children), 7.5". *Courtesy of Adobe Gallery.*

Suina, Buffy Cordero. Cochiti, Male storyteller (4 children), 7". *Courtesy of Adobe Gallery.*

Suina, Buffy Cordero. Cochiti, Male storyteller (11 children), 1989, 10.75". *Courtesy of Adobe Gallery.*

Suina, Carol. Cochiti, Female storyteller (10 children), 9.25. *Courtesy of Indian Traders West.*

Suina, D. (Water Fox). Cochiti, Male storyteller (6 children), 7". *Courtesy of Palms Trading Company.*

Suina, D. Cochiti, Mudhead (2 children), 4". *Courtesy of Palms Trading Company.*

Suina, D. (Water Fox). Cochiti, Male storyteller (4 children), 5". *Courtesy of Palms Trading Company.*

Suina, Dena M. Cochiti, Female storyteller (11 children), 6.25″. *Courtesy of Andrews Pueblo Gallery.*

Suina, E.K. & Blooming Flower. Cochiti, Females, l-r: 5.5″, 6.5″, 7.5″. *Courtesy of Palms Trading Company.*

Suina, Grace. Cochiti, Female, 5". *Courtesy of Bing Crosby's.*

Suina, J. Cochiti, Male storyteller (4 children), 5.5". *Courtesy of Palms Trading Company.*

Suina, Joseph D. Cochiti, Female storyteller (9 children). *Courtesy of Palms Trading Company.*

Suina, Louise E. Cochiti, Corn maiden, 7.5". *Courtesy of Andrews Pueblo Gallery.*

Suina, Louise. Cochiti, Female storyteller (8 children). *Courtesy of Adobe Gallery.*

Suina, Marie C. Cochiti, Nativity (12 piece), 4.25". *Courtesy of The Kiva.*

Suina, Marie. Cochiti, l: male (4 children); r: female (4 children). *Courtesy of Indian Post.*

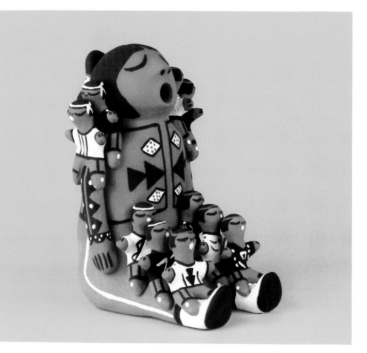

Suina, N. (Water Fox). Cochiti, Male storyteller (10 children), 7". *Courtesy of Palms Trading Company.*

Suina, N. Cochiti, Male storyteller (4 children), 5". *Courtesy of Palms Trading Company.*

Suina, T.T. (Water Fox). Cochiti,
Male storyteller (10 children), 7".
Courtesy of Palms Trading Company.

Suina, N. Cochiti-Hopi, Female storyteller (16 children), 10.25".
Courtesy of a private collection.

Trancosa, Del. Cochiti, Turtle (2 children), 8".
Courtesy of Adobe Gallery.

Trujillo, D. Cochiti, male (4 children). *Courtesy of Indian Post.*

Trancosa, Del. Cochiti, Male storyteller (4 children), 9". *Courtesy of Adobe Gallery.*

Trujillo, D. Cochiti, Drummer (4 children), 5".
Courtesy of a private collection.

Trujillo, D. Cochiti, Male storyteller (29 children), 12.5". *Courtesy of Palms Trading Company.*

Trujillo, D. Cochiti, Nativity (11 piece). *Courtesy of Palms Trading Company.*

Trujillo, D. Cochiti, Male storyteller (10 children, 1 dog), 8.75". *Courtesy of Palms Trading Company.*

Trujillo, David. Cochiti, Female storyteller (4 children), 6". *Courtesy of Palms Trading Company.*

Trujillo, Dorothy. Cochiti, Males (l: 16 children; r: 40 children), l: 10"; r: 11". *Courtesy of a private collection.*

Trujillo, Dorothy. Cochiti, Female storyteller (1 child), 1981. *Courtesy of Adobe Gallery.*

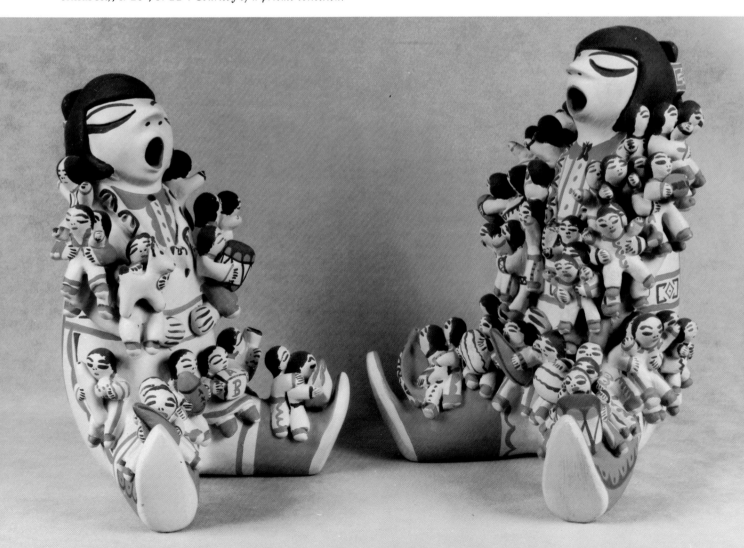

Trujillo, Mary and Leonard. Cochiti, Angel with corn. *Courtesy of Andrews Pueblo Gallery.*

Trujillo, Felipa. Cochiti, Females. *Courtesy of Adobe Gallery.*

Trujillo, Geri. Cochiti, Turtle (3 children), 5.75". *Courtesy of Andrews Pueblo Gallery.*

Trujillo, Mary and Leonard. Cochiti, Bear (4 cubs), 11". *Courtesy of Andrews Pueblo Gallery.*

Trujillo, Mary and Leonard. Cochiti, Male story-teller (8 children), 11.25". *Courtesy of Andrews Pueblo Gallery.*

Trujillo, Mary. Cochiti, Smoking figure, 1989, 12.5". *Courtesy of Adobe Gallery.*

Trujillo, Mary and Leonard. Cochiti, Drummer, 8.25". *Courtesy of Andrews Pueblo Gallery.*

44

Trujillo, Mary. Cochiti, Female storyteller (7 children), 10.5". *Courtesy of Foutz Trading Company.*

Trujillo, Mary and Leonard. Cochiti, Female storyteller (2 children), 11.25". *Courtesy of Andrews Pueblo Gallery.*

Trujillo, Mary. Cochiti, Drummer, 13". *Courtesy of Foutz Trading Company.*

Trujillo, Rufina. Cochiti, Female storyteller (2 children), 4". *Courtesy of Adobe Gallery.*

Van Pelt, M. Cochiti, Figure, 1989, 4.5". *Courtesy of Palms Trading Company.*

Valdo, M. Cochiti, Male and Female Figures, 5". *Courtesy of Palms Trading Company.*

Valencia, C. Cochiti, Nativity (10 piece). *Courtesy of Palms Trading Company.*

Bonham, A.L. Cochiti-Santa Fe, Rabbit (4 bunnies), 13.25". *Courtesy of The Kiva.*

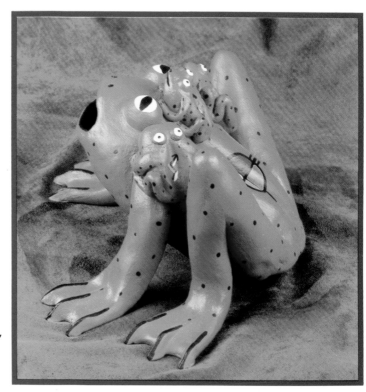

Bonham, Alice L.. Cochiti-Santa Fe, Frog (3 froglets), 5.25". *Courtesy of The Kiva.*

Aragon, Wanda. Acoma, Female storyteller (3 children), 1986. *Courtesy of Adobe Gallery.*

Biea, Nellie. Acoma, Owl. *Courtesy of Adobe Gallery.*

Chino, S. Acoma, Nativity (11 piece). *Courtesy of Palms Trading Company.*

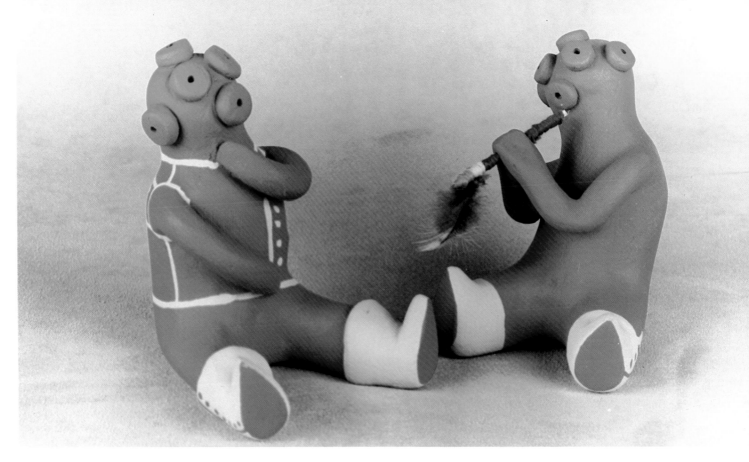

Concha, J.R. Acoma, Mudheads, 4". *Courtesy of Palms Trading Company.*

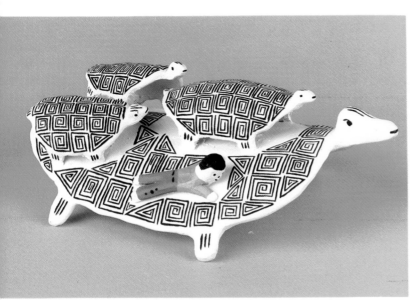

Garcia, C. Acoma, Turtle (3 turtles & 2 children), 3". *Courtesy of Palms Trading Company.*

Henderson, M. Acoma, Pot (5 children), 8.25". *Courtesy of a private collection.*

49

Henderson, Marilyn. Acoma, Female storyteller
(13 children), 9.5". *Courtesy of Andrews Pueblo
Gallery.*

Henderson, Marilyn. Acoma, Female storyteller (2 children). *Courtesy of Adobe Gallery.*

Henderson, Marilyn. Acoma, Storytellers, l: 5.125"; r: 4.125". *Courtesy of Andrews Pueblo Gallery.*

Henderson, Marilyn. Acoma, Male story-teller (1 child), 2". *Courtesy of Adobe Gallery.*

Henderson, Marilyn. Acoma, Boys fishing, 3.25. *Courtesy of Andrews Pueblo Gallery.*

51

Juanico, Marie S. Acoma, Male storyteller (many children), 1981, 6". *Courtesy of Adobe Gallery (photo: William L. Rada).*

Lewis, K. Acoma, Female storyteller (2 children), 3.75". *Courtesy of Palms Trading Company.*

L., Joyce. Acoma, Nativity (9 piece). *Courtesy of Palms Trading Company.*

Lydia. Acoma, Male storyteller (many children), 11.5". *Courtesy of Bing Crosby's.*

Sanchez, M. Acoma , Turtle (two babies), 2".
Courtesy of Adobe Gallery.

Pino, Frances Torivio. Acoma, Female storyteller
(10 children), 1986. *Courtesy of Adobe Gallery.*

Shields, Ethel. Acoma, Female storyteller (6
children), 1986. *Courtesy of Adobe Gallery.*

Shutiva, Jackie. Acoma, Owl. *Courtesy of Adobe
Gallery.*

Torivio, R.H. Acoma, Owl (2 owlets), 9.5".
Courtesy of a private collection.

Vallo, Darlene L. . Acoma, Female storyteller (4 children), 3.5". *Courtesy of Palms Trading Company.*

Vallo, Darlene. Acoma, Female storyteller (6 children), 5.75". *Courtesy of Palms Trading Company.*

Vallo, Raphael. Acoma, Male storyteller (2 children), 1985, 4.25". *Courtesy of Andrews Pueblo Gallery.*

SANTO DOMINGO

A.L. Santo Domingo, Corn figures, 3.25"-4". *Courtesy of Jim Silva.*

Towa Pueblo

Armijo, C. Jemez, Female, 8". *Courtesy of Bing Crosby's.*

G.C. Jemez, Female storyteller (6 children), 11". *Courtesy of Wind River Trading Company.*

Cajero, Anita. Jemez, "Mom and Dad", 5.5". *Courtesy of Palms Trading Company.*

Cajero, Anita. Jemez, Male storyteller (3 children), 3.5". *Courtesy of Palms Trading Company.*

Cajero, Anita. Jemez, Female storyteller (3 children), 4". *Courtesy of Palms Trading Company.*

Cajero, E. (Bird Image). Jemez, "Far Star" figure, 9.75". *Courtesy of Palms Trading Company.*

Cajero, E. (Bird Image). Jemez, "Corn Dancer", 11". *Courtesy of Palms Trading Company.*

Cajero, E. (Bird Image). Jemez, "Cornflower" Female (4 children). *Courtesy of Palms Trading Company.*

Cajero, E. (Bird Image). Jemez, "Sunflower", female (33 children), 13". *Courtesy of Palms Trading Company.*

D.Y.C. Jemez, Male and female, 5". *Courtesy of Indian Traders West.*

D.Y.C. Back of above photo.

Chinana. Jemez, Nativity (6 pieces), 9". *Courtesy of Indian Traders West.*

Chinana. Jemez, Nativity (9 piece). *Courtesy of Palms Trading Company.*

Chinana. Jemez, Nativity (9 pieces). *Courtesy of The Kiva.*

Chinana. Jemez, Female, 4". *Courtesy of Bing Crosby's.*

Chosa, P. Jemez, Female storyteller (4 children), 5.25". *Courtesy of Palms Trading Company.*

Chosa, P. Jemez, Owls, l: 9.75"; r: 6.75". *Courtesy of Jim Silva.*

Chosa, P. Jemez, Storytellers, 5"-5.5". *Courtesy of Jim Silva.*

Chosa, P. Jemez, Storytellers, 5". *Courtesy of Jim Silva.*

Chosa, P. Jemez, Males and Female, 4.25". *Courtesy of Palms Trading Company.*

Chosa, Pat. Jemez, Nativity (5 piece), 4". *Courtesy of Jim Silva.*

Colleteta, Andrea. Jemez, Storytellers, 4"-4.5".
Courtesy of Palms Trading Company.

Colleteta, V. Jemez, Cornfigure, 3/5". *Courtesy of Palms Trading Company.*

Colleteta, V. Jemez, Male storyteller (8 children), 7". *Courtesy of Palms Trading Company.*

Coriz, Marie E. Jemez, Male storyteller (8 children), 11". *Courtesy of Palms Trading Company.*

K.G.E. Jemez, Female storyteller (6 children). *Courtesy of Palms Trading Company.*

K.G.E. Jemez, Females. *Courtesy of Palms Trading Company.*

Eteeyan, Kimberly G.. Jemez, Female storyteller (4 children), 3.75". *Courtesy of Adobe Gallery.*

Fragua, C. (aged 12). Jemez, Female storyteller (3 children), 3.5". *Courtesy of Foutz Trading Company.*

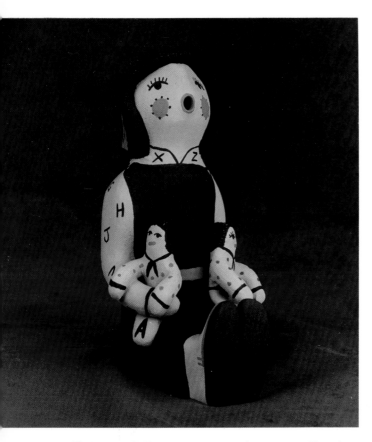

Fragua, C.K. Jemez, Female storyteller (2 children), 6.25". *Courtesy of Wind River Trading Company.*

Fragua, C.K. Jemez, Female storyteller (5 children), 1989, 9.75". *Courtesy of Wind River Trading Company.*

Fragua, C.K. Jemez, Clown (4 children), 1989, 10.25". *Courtesy of Wind River Trading Company.*

Fragua, Emily. Jemez, Clown (2 children). *Courtesy of Adobe Gallery.*

Fragua, F. Jemez, Females, Taller: 6.5". *Courtesy of Turquoise Lady.*

Fragua, F. (r), Fragua, A. (aged 10) (l). Jemez, Turtles, Taller: 5.25". *Courtesy of Turquoise Lady.*

Fragua, Grace L. Jemez, two story tellers and an ashtray, 1977. *Courtesy of C.F. Gachupin.*

Fragua, J. Jemez, Bear (2 cubs), 4.75". *Courtesy of Turquoise Lady.*

66

Fragua, Jan. Jemez, Female storyteller (6 children), 7". *Courtesy of Turquoise Lady.*

Fragua, J.L. Jemez, Clown (1 child, 3 watermelons), 10.75". *Courtesy of Wind River Trading Company.*

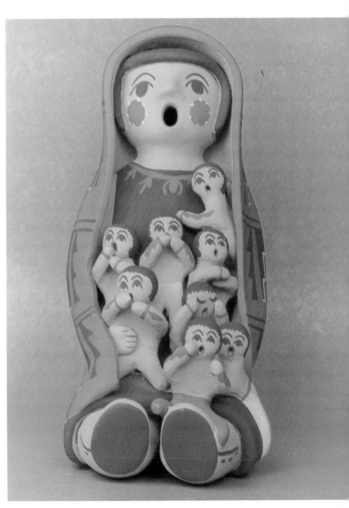

Fragua, Linda Lucero. Jemez, Female, 9". *Courtesy of Bing Crosby's.*

Fragua, R. Jemez, Turtle (2 children), 3.5″. *Courtesy of Indian Traders West.*

Fragua, Rose T. Jemez, Clown Tree, 1986. *Courtesy C.F. Gachupin.*

Fragua, P. Jemez, Female storyteller (4 children), 5.5″. *Courtesy of Palms Trading Company.*

Gachupin, C.F. Jemez, Cornfigure, 9″. *Courtesy of Adobe Gallery.*

Gachupin, C. Jemez, Females, 1989, l-r: 5.5″, 6.375″, 6.125″. *Courtesy of Indian Traders West.*

68

Gachupin, Caroline Fragua. Jemez, Female storyteller (3 children), 1981. *Courtesy of Adobe Gallery.*

Gachupin, Caroline F. Jemez, Female storyteller (3 children). *Courtesy of Adobe Gallery.*

Gachupin, Caroline F. Jemez, Female storyteller (3 children). *Courtesy of Adobe Gallery.*

Gachupin, Caroline F. Jemez, Female storyteller (10 children). *Courtesy of Adobe Gallery.*

Gachupin, Henrietta Toya. Jemez, Male storyteller (7 children), 8". *Courtesy of Palms Trading Company.*

Gachupin, Caroline F. Jemez, Coyote (2 pups), 7". *Courtesy of Brett Bastien.*

Gachupin, Joseph. Jemez, "Corn Family", 6-7". *Courtesy of Palms Trading Company.*

Gachupin, Joseph. Jemez, Corn figures, 7.5", 6.5". *Courtesy of Indian Traders West.*

Gachupin, Laura. Jemez, Cornmaiden and Owl, l: 2.75";
r: 9.125". *Courtesy of Andrews Pueblo Gallery.*

Gachupin, Laura. Jemez, Group, 7.75". *Courtesy of Bing
Crosby's.*

Gachupin, P. Jemez, Female storyteller (9
children), 8.75". *Courtesy of a private collection.*

72

Gachupin, Persingula. Jemez, Nativity (14 pieces). *(Courtesy of Andrews Pueblo Gallery.)*

Gachupin, Persingula, M. Jemez, Female story-teller (8 children), 1986. *Courtesy of Adobe Gallery.*

Gachupin, W. Jemez, Female storyteller (12 children), 9". *Courtesy of Palms Trading Company.*

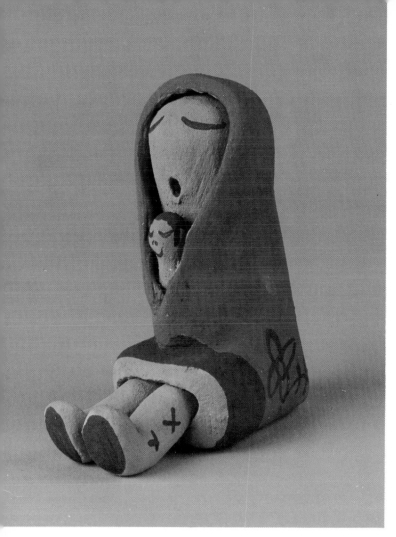

P.H. Jemez, Female storyteller (1 child), 4". *Courtesy of Palms Trading Company.*

Loretto, Alma Concha. Jemez, Male, 9". *Courtesy of Bing Crosby's.*

J.L. Jemez, Storytellers, 6". *Courtesy of Palms Trading Company.*

T.L. Jemez, Nativity. *Courtesy of Palms Trading Company.*

Loretto, Alma Concha. Jemez, Nativity (14 piece), 8" (angel). *Courtesy of Adobe Gallery.*

Loretto, B. Jemez, Male storyteller (4 children), 5". *Courtesy of Palms Trading Company.*

Loretto, F. Jemez, Females, 7.5". *Courtesy of Palms Trading Company.*

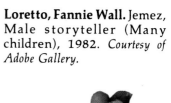

Loretto, F. Jemez, Nativity (9 piece), 5". *Courtesy of Palms Trading Company.*

Loretto, Fannie Wall. Jemez, Male storyteller (Many children), 1982. *Courtesy of Adobe Gallery.*

Loretto, Fannie. Jemez, Clown drummer. *Courtesy of The Kiva.*

Loretto, Natalie. Jemez, Male storyteller (3 children), 3.5". *Courtesy of Palms Trading Company.*

Loretto, Felicia. Jemez, Female storyteller (12 children), 8.75". *Courtesy of Palms Trading Company.*

Loretto, V. & J. Jemez, Male storyteller (8 children), 5.25". *Courtesy of Indian Traders West.*

Loretto, Debbie Seonia. Jemez, Male storyteller (5 children), 4". *Courtesy of Palms Trading Company.*

Lucero, L. Lupe Loretto. Jemez, Female storyteller (15 children), 11/5". *Courtesy of Andrews Pueblo Gallery.*

Lucero, L. Lupe Loretto . Jemez, Mudhead (8 children), 7". *Courtesy of Palms Trading Company.*

Lucero, L. Lupe Loretto. Jemez, Female storyteller (6 children), 8". *Courtesy of Palms Trading Company.*

Lucero, L. Lupe Loretto. Jemez, Mudhead (12 children), 10.25". *Courtesy of Turquoise Lady.*

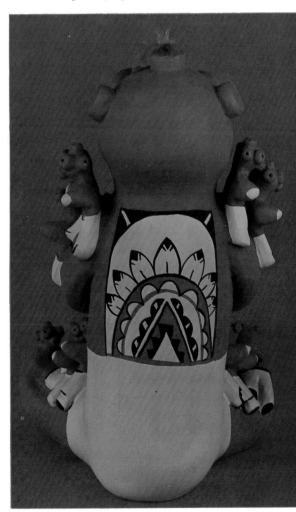

Lucero, L. Lupe Lorretto. Back view of left photo.

P.M. Jemez, Female storyteller (4 children), 3.5". *Courtesy of Palms Trading Company.*

Lucero, Linda. Jemez, Koshare Clown (2 chldren), 1980, 7.75". *Courtesy of Adobe Gallery. (photo: William L. Rada).*

Lucero, William. Jemez, Female storyteller (18 children), 8.5". *Courtesy of Brett Bastien.*

Madalena, M. Jemez, Female storyteller (5 children), 7". *Courtesy of Wind River Trading Company.*

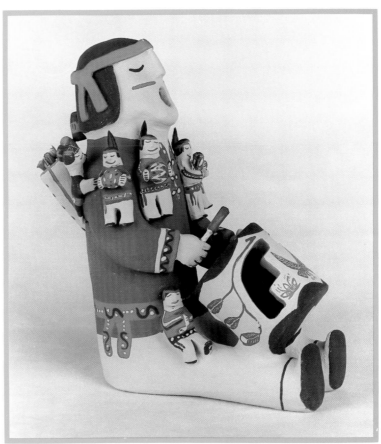

Madalena, M. Jemez, Bottle with head stopper, 8". *Courtesy of Palms Trading Company.*

Magdalena, D.J. Jemez, Male Drummer (7 children), 6.75". *Courtesy of Palms Trading Company.*

Madalena, M. Jemez, Females, 9". *Courtesy of Palms Trading Company.*

Panana, Reyes. Jemez, Mudhead clown (2 children), 10.375". *Courtesy of Indian Traders West.*

Pecos, Carol. Jemez, Female storyteller (19 children), 1986. *Courtesy of Adobe Gallery.*

Panana, Reyes. Jemez, Mudheads. *Courtesy of Palms Trading Company.*

Pecos, Carol. Jemez, Male storyteller (1 child), 3.75". *Courtesy of Bing Crosby's.*

Pecos, Carol. Jemez, Female storyteller (4 children), 5". *Courtesy of Palms Trading Company.*

Pecos, Carol. Jemez, Cornfigure, 4". *Courtesy of Andrews Pueblo Gallery.*

Rhodes, Rose Pecos Sun. Jemez, Females(l: 4 children; r: 11 children & 1 dog), l: 3"; r: 8". *Courtesy of Bing Crosby's.*

Rhodes, Rose Pecos Sun. Jemez, Female story-teller (8 children), 1986. *Courtesy of Adobe Gallery.*

Romero, Maria G. Jemez, Female storytellers, l: 4.625"; r: 6". *Courtesy of Andrews Pueblo Gallery.*

Romero, Marie G. Jemez, Mocassin (16 children), 10". *Courtesy of Adobe Gallery.*

Sabaquie. Jemez, Storytellers, 5.5". *Courtesy of Palms Trading Company.*

S.T.S. Jemez, Male storyteller (6 children), 1987, 6.5". *Courtesy of Wind River Trading Company.*

Sabaquie. Jemez, Male storyteller (7 children), 5". *Courtesy of Palms Trading Company.*

Sando, Carolyn. Jemez, Female storyteller (8 children), 4.5". *Courtesy of Palms Trading Company.*

Sando, C. Jemez, Female storyteller (8 children). *Courtesy of Bing Crosby's.*

Sando, Carolyn. Jemez, Storytellers, l-r: 2.5", 5", 19.5". *Courtesy of Wind River Trading Company.*

Sando, C. Jemez, Nativity (8 piece), 6". *Courtesy of Palms Trading Company.*

Sando, D. Jemez, Female storyteller (21 children), 12.5". *Courtesy of Palms Trading Company.*

Sando, K. Jemez, Female storyteller (about 90 children), 21". *Courtesy of Palms Trading Company.*

Sando, T. Jemez, Female storyteller (6 children), 6.5". *Courtesy of Palms Trading Company.*

Sando, T. Jemez, Wedding Jar (5 children). *Courtesy of Palms Trading Company.*

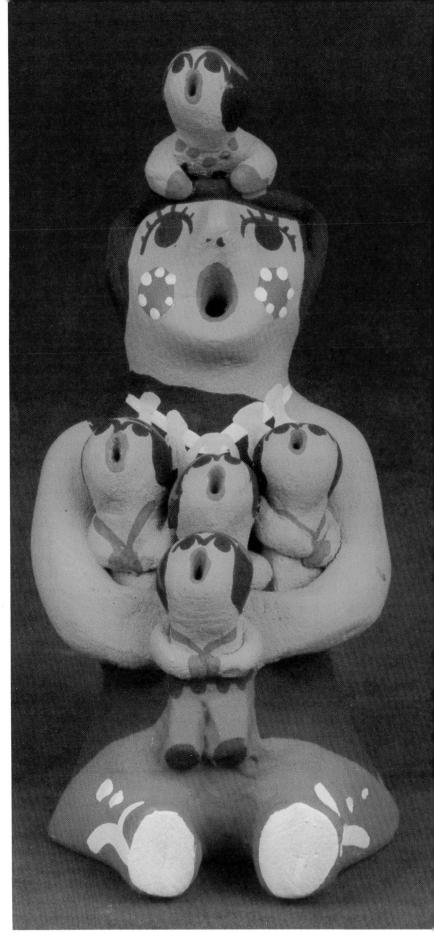

Sando, T. Jemez, Female storyteller (4 children). *Courtesy of Wind River Trading Company.*

Santana, Seonia. Jemez, Female storyteller (6 children), 5″. *Courtesy of Palms Trading Company.*

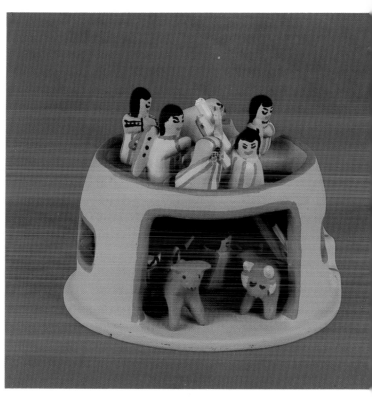

Seonia, Caroline L. Jemez, Group in round house. *Courtesy of Palms Trading Company.*

Seonia, Caroline L. Jemez, Male storyteller (6 children). *Courtesy of Palms Trading Company.*

Seonia, Caroline L. Jemez, Male storyteller (10 children), 8.75″. *Courtesy of Palms Trading Company.*

Seonia, Caroline L. Jemez, Female storyteller (11 children), 10". *Courtesy of Palms Trading Company.*

Shendo, J.S. Jemez, Female storyteller (5 children), 4". *Courtesy of Palms Trading Company.*

Shendo, J.S. Jemez, Male and Female, 4.75". *Courtesy of Palms Trading Company.*

Shije, Adrienne. Jemez, Female storyteller (4 children), 4.25". *Courtesy of Palms Trading Company.*

Shije, Adrienne. Jemez, Female storyteller (3 children), 4". *Courtesy of Palms Trading Company.*

Small, Mary. Jemez, Female storyteller (13 children), 1988, 9.75". *Courtesy of Palms Trading Company.*

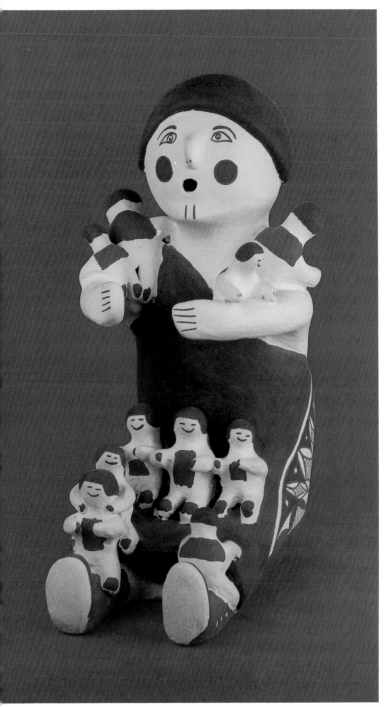

Small, Mary. Jemez, Female storyteller (10 children), 11.25". *Courtesy of Jim Silva.*

Toledo, D. Jemez, Male storyteller (5 children), 1988, 6". *Courtesy of Palms Trading Company.*

Toledo, L. Jemez, Male, 5.25". *Courtesy of Bing Crosby's.*

Tosa, Edwina. Jemez, Male storyteller (6 children), 7.5". *Courtesy of Wind River Trading Company.*

Tortalita, Edwina Tosa. Jemez, Clown (1 child), 7.5". *Courtesy of Wind River Trading Company.*

Tosa, Persingula R. Jemez, Female storyteller (9 children), 7.5". *Courtesy of Palms Trading Company.*

Toya, Anita F. Jemez, Cornfigure (4 children), 8.5". *Courtesy of Palms Trading Company.*

Toya, Anita F. Jemez, Clown (10 children), 12". *Courtesy of Andrews Pueblo Gallery.*

Toya, B. Jemez, Female storyteller (8 children), 5.5". *Courtesy of Palms Trading Company.*

Toya, B.G. Jemez, Female storyteller (1 child), 3″.
Courtesy of Palms Trading Company.

Toya, Damian. Jemez, Female storyteller (1 child), 8″.
Courtesy of Palms Trading Company.

Toya, D. Jemez, Nativity (7 piece). *Courtesy of Palms Trading Company.*

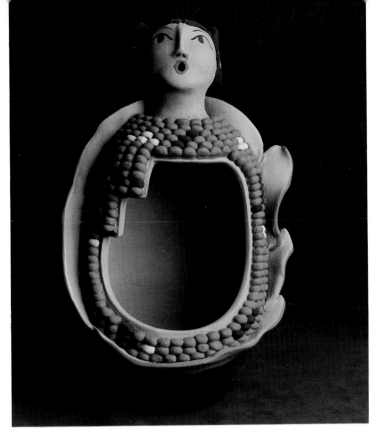

Toya, J.F. Jemez, Cornfigure, 14.5". *Courtesy of Wind River Trading Company.*

Toya, Judy. Jemez, Female storyteller (6 children), 6". *Courtesy of Palms Trading Company.*

Toya, Judy. Jemez, Male storyteller (5 children), 8". *Courtesy of Palms Trading Company.*

Toya, K.F. Jemez, Female storyteller (4 children), 7.5". *Courtesy of Palms Trading Company.*

Toya, Loretto. Jemez, Nativity (4 pieces). *Courtesy of Palms Trading Company.*

Toya, Lyda. Jemez, Female storyteller (6 children), 5.5". *Courtesy of Palms Trading Company.*

Toya, M. Ellen. Jemez, Nativity (11 piece), 6.75". *Courtesy of Palms Trading Company.*

Toya, Marie Ellen. Jemez, Nativity (7 piece). *Courtesy of Palms Trading Company.*

Toya, Marie. Jemez, Nativity (11 piece). *Courtesy of Palms Trading Company.*

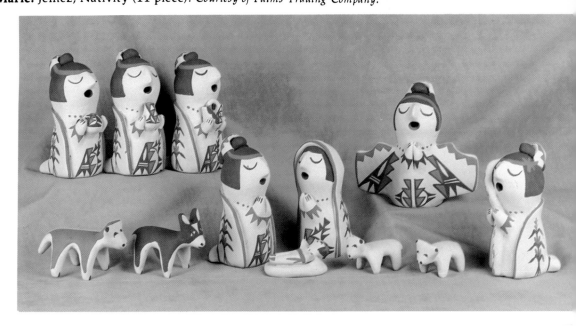

Toya, Mary Ellen. Jemez, Nativity (12 piece), 6.75". *Courtesy of Palms Trading Company.*

Toya, Mary Ellen. Jemez, Female storyteller (6 children), 6.25". *Courtesy of Palms Trading Company.*

Toya, Mary Ellen. Jemez, Male storyteller (18 children), 10". *Courtesy of Andrews Pueblo Gallery.*

Toya, Mary Ellen. Jemez, Clown (10 children), 13.5". *Courtesy of The Kiva.*

Toya, Mary E. Jemez, Female storyteller (4 children), 6.25". *Courtesy of Palms Trading Company.*

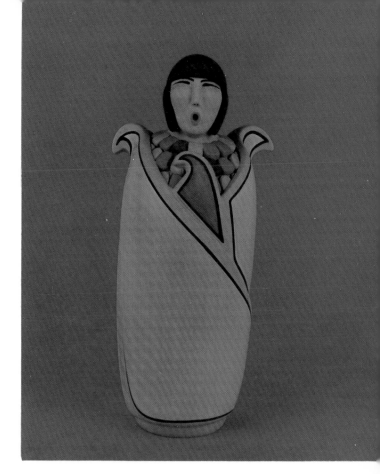

Toya, Maxine. Jemez, Cornfigure, 9.5". *Courtesy of Andrews Pueblo Gallery.*

Toya, Maxine. Jemez, Standing figures, 6.75". *Courtesy of Andrews Pueblo Gallery.*

Toya, Maxine. Jemez, Female storyteller (1 child), 1981. *Courtesy of Adobe Gallery.*

101

Toya, R.F. Jemez, Nativity (10 piece), 4.5″. *Courtesy of Palms Trading Company.*

Toya, Rosa Lee. Jemez, Female storyteller (3 children), 4.5″. *Courtesy of Palms Trading Company.*

Toya, Yolanda. Jemez, Female storyteller (6 children), 6.625″. *Courtesy of Andrews Pueblo Gallery.*

Toya. Jemez, Male and Female, 10". *Courtesy of Palms Trading Company.*

Toya. Jemez, Corn-figure (3 children), 6.5". *Courtesy of Palms Trading Company.*

Toya. Jemez, Female storyteller (5 children), 6". *Courtesy of Palms Trading Company.*

Toya. Jemez, Female storyteller (25 children), 1989, 10.75". *Courtesy of Palms Trading Company.*

Tsosie, E. Fragua. Jemez, Storytellers, 9". *Courtesy of The Kiva.*

Tsosie, E.F. Jemez, Female storyteller (14 children), 7.75". *Courtesy of a private collection.*

Tsosie, E. Jemez, Clown (2 children), 8.75". *Courtesy of a private collection.*

Tsosie, E. Jemez, Frog (4 froglets), 10.5". *Courtesy of Jim Silva.*

Tsosie, E. Jemez, Female storyteller (15 children)". *Courtesy of Palms Trading Company.*

Tsosie, E. Jemez, Nativity (7 piece), 5.25". *Courtesy of Turquoise Lady.*

Tsosie, Leonard. Jemez, Clown drummer, 5.75".
Courtesy of Wind River Trading Company.

Tsosie, Lucy. Jemez, Male storyteller (3 children), 7.5". *Courtesy of Palms Trading Company.*

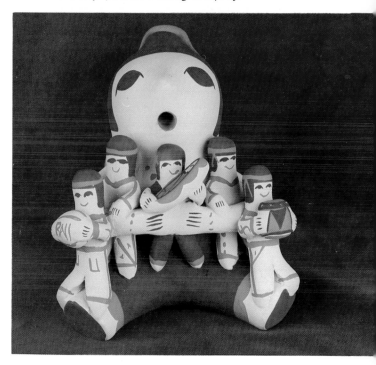

Waquiri, Pauline. Jemez, Female, c. 1985, 3.75".
Courtesy of Armand and Barbara Winfield.

Waquie, C. Jemez, Male storyteller (6 children), 5.75". *Courtesy of Palms Trading Company.*

Waquiri, Katherine. Jemez, Female storyteller (8 children), c. 1985, 7.25". *Courtesy of Armand and Barbara Winfield.*

Yepa, B. Jemez, Cornfigure (4 children), 7". *Courtesy of Palms Trading Company.*

Waquiri, Pauline. Jemez, Female, c. 1985, 3.75". *Courtesy of Armand and Barbara Winfield.*

Yepa, Bessie. Jemez, Cornfigure (2 children), 6". *Courtesy of Palms Trading Company.*

Concha, Antoinette. Jemez-Taos, Mudhead drummer, 5.25". *Courtesy of Wind River Trading Company.*

Concha, Antoinette. Jemez-Taos, Mudhead (12 children), 1989. *Courtesy of Wind River Trading Company.*

Concha, Antoinette. Jemez-Taos, Mudheads (1989). *Courtesy of Indian Post.*

Tewa Pueblos

Vigil, Art. Tesuque, Female storyteller (7 children), 1986. *Courtesy of Adobe Gallery.*

Pino, Loreneita. Tesuque, Rain god, c. 1985, 6.25". *Courtesy of Armand and Barbara Winfield.*

Vigil, Art. Tesuque, Hanging angels, 1988. *Courtesy of Adobe Gallery.*

Vigil, Manuel. Tesuque, Nativity. *Courtesy of Adobe Gallery.*

Vigil, Manuel. Tesuque, Nativity. *Courtesy of Adobe Gallery.*

Vigil, Manuel. Detail of photo above.

NAMBE

Herrera, Marie. Nambe, Female storyteller (5 children), 7". *Courtesy of Adobe Gallery.*

SAN JUAN

Garcia, Reycita. San Juan, Grandparents (5 children), 4". *Courtesy of Palms Trading Company.*

SAN ILDEFONSO

Martinez, Charlene. San Ildefonso, Mudhead (1 child), 1986. *Courtesy of Adobe Gallery.*

Yellowbird. San Ildefonso, Nativity (6 piece), 5". *Courtesy of Adobe Gallery.*

SANTA CLARA

Gallagea, Joyce Sisceros. Santa Clara, Coyote (4 pups), 11.25". *Courtesy of The Kiva.*

Gallagea, Joyce Sisceros. Santa Clara, Female storyteller (3 children), 6.5". *Courtesy of The Kiva.*

Gutierrez, Dorothy and Paul. Santa Clara, Storytellers, 3.5". *Courtesy of Andrews Pueblo Gallery.*

Gutierrez, Dorothy and Paul. Santa Clara, Nativity (13 piece), 3.5". *Courtesy of Palms Trading Company.*

Gutierrez, Dorothy and Paul. Santa Clara, Nativity (7 piece), 1985. *Courtesy of Adobe Gallery.*

Gutierrez, Dorothy & Paul. Santa Clara, Mudhead (6 children). *Courtesy of Adobe Gallery.*

Gutierrez, Dorothy and Paul. Santa Clara, Nativity (9 piece). *Courtesy of Palms Trading Company.*

Gutierrez, Gary. Santa Clara, Male storyteller (1 mudhead), 4". *Courtesy of Andrews Pueblo Gallery.*

Gutierrez, Margaret & Luther. Santa Clara, Mudhead (9 children), 1986. *Courtesy of Adobe Gallery.*

Gutierrez, Margaret and Luther. Santa Clara, Female storyteller (6 children), 1986. *Courtesy of Adobe Gallery.*

Gutierrez, Margaret & Luther. Santa Clara, Nativity (17 piece). *Courtesy of Adobe Gallery.*

Lorento, Rose. Santa Clara, Frog group, Tallest: 12". *Courtesy of The Kiva.*

Mirabel, Martha. Santa Clara, Nativity (6 piece). *Courtesy of Adobe Gallery.*

Naranjo, Maria. Santa Clara, Ark (18 figures), 9".
Courtesy of Adobe Gallery.

Naranjo, Maria. Santa Clara, Male storyteller (6 children), 8.5". *Courtesy of Adobe Gallery.*

Petiras, Margaret. Santa Clara, Balloon (3 clowns), 1989, 12". *Courtesy of Adobe Gallery.*

Teba, J. Santa Clara, Nativity (8 pieces), 3.5". *Courtesy of Indian Traders West.*

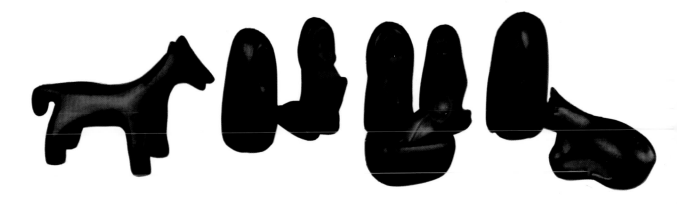

Tiwa Pueblos

Cheyenne Jim. Taos, Male storyteller (Micaceous clay), 10". *Courtesy of The Kiva.*

Cheyenne Jim. Taos, Female, 8.5". *Courtesy of Bing Crosby's.*

Dandova, Juan. Taos, Nativity (6 piece), 11.5". *Courtesy of Keams Canyon Trading Post.*

Garcia, L. Taos, Female story-teller. *Courtesy of Bing Crosby's.*

Cheyenne Jim. Taos, Nativity (16 pieces), 7.5". *Courtesy of The Kiva.*

Lujan-Hauer, Pam. Taos, Female storyteller (2 children), 1986. *Courtesy of Adobe Gallery.*

Quintana, Margaret. Taos, Female storyteller (4 children), 5.25". *Courtesy of Palms Trading Company.*

Sandoval, Juan. Taos, Male figure, 6.25". *Courtesy of a private collection.*

Martinez, Juanita. Taos, Male storyteller (8 children), 6.5". *Courtesy of Palms Trading Company.*

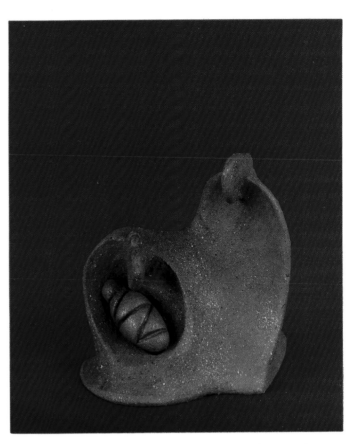

Sandoval, Juan. Taos, Figure on horse, 6.75".
Courtesy of the Kiva.

Suazo, Sharon. Taos, Nativity (1 piece), 4".
Courtesy of Turquoise Lady.

Suazo, Sharon. Taos, Nativity (4 piece). *Courtesy of Palms Trading Company.*

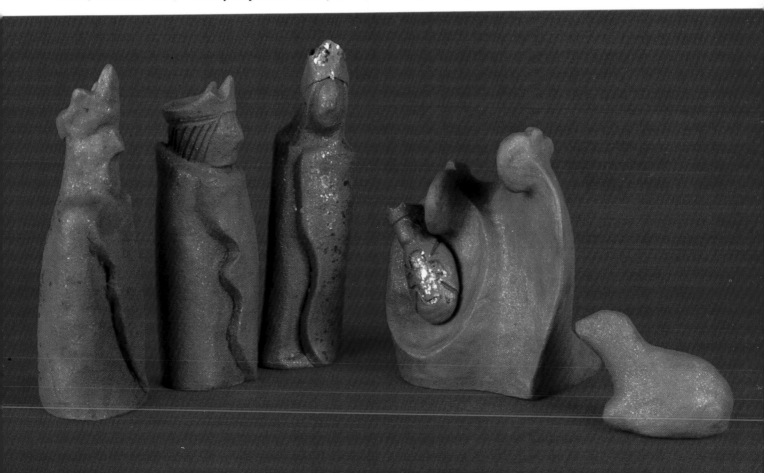

ISLETA

Teller, Chris. Isleta, Nativity (7 piece). *Courtesy of Palms Trading Company.*

Teller, Chris. Isleta, Females, 4-5". *Courtesy of Palms Trading Company.*

Teller, Chris. Isleta, Nativity (7 piece). *Courtesy of Palms Trading Company.*

Teller, Lynette. Isleta, Storytellers, 2.75", 4.25". *Courtesy of Adobe Gallery.*

Teller, Mona. Isleta, Female storyteller (4 children), 1986. *Courtesy of Adobe Gallery.*

Teller, Mona. Isleta, Nativity (7 pieces), 5.5". *Courtesy of The Kiva.*

Teller, Mona. Isleta, Female storytellers, 4.5"-5.25". *Courtesy of Palms Trading Company.*

Teller, Mona. Isleta, Nativity (9 piece), 5.5". *Courtesy of Palms Trading Company.*

Teller, Robin. Isleta, Storytellers, 3", 4.75". *Courtesy of Adobe Gallery.*

Teller, Robin. Isleta, Female storyteller (7 children). *Courtesy of Adobe Gallery.*

Teller, Robin. Isleta, Female storyteller (8 children). *Courtesy of Adobe Gallery.*

Teller, Robin. Isleta, Female storyteller (11 children), 1988. *Courtesy of Adobe Gallery.*

Teller, Robin. Isleta, Female storyteller (13 children), 7.25". *Courtesy of Adobe Gallery.*

Teller, Stella. Isleta, Nativity. *Courtesy of Indian Post.*

Teller, Stella. Isleta, Nativity (12 piece).
Courtesy of Adobe Gallery.

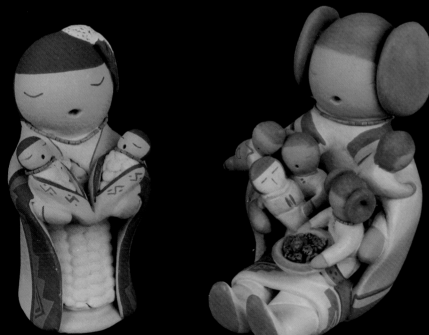

Teller, Stella. Isleta, Female storyteller (11 children), 1988. *Courtesy of Adobe Gallery.*

Teller, Stella. Isleta, Storytellers, l: 5"; r: 5.25".
Courtesy of Adobe Gallery.

Teller, Stella. Isleta, Nativity (12 pieces), 1989. *Courtesy of Adobe Gallery.*

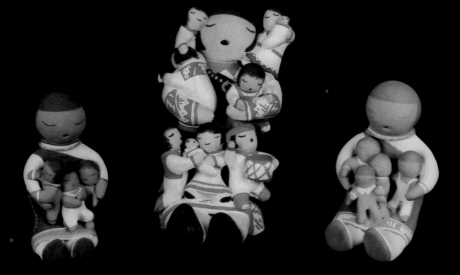

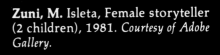

Zuni, M. Isleta, Female storyteller (2 children), 1981. *Courtesy of Adobe Gallery.*

Teller, Stella. Isleta, Females (center figure is older). *Courtesy of Indian Post.*

LAGUNA

DeVore, Rose. Laguna, Female story-teller (3 children). *Courtesy of Adobe Gallery.*

DeVore, Rose. Laguna, Female storyteller (7 children). *Courtesy of Adobe Gallery.*

DeVore, Rose. Laguna, Female story-teller (3 children). *Courtesy of Adobe Gallery.*

Padilla, Andrew. Laguna, Turtle (3 babies). *Courtesy of Adobe Gallery.*

Dallas, Tony. Hopi, Mudhead figures. *Courtesy of Indian Post.*

Dallas, Tony. Hopi, Mudhead (4 children), 5.5".
Courtesy of Adobe Gallery.

Dallas, Tony. Hopi, Mudhead (4 children), 10".
Courtesy of The Kiva.

Sakenima, Norma. Hopi, Storytellers, l: 9.5"; r: 10.25". *Courtesy of Jim Silva.*

Sakenima, Norma. Hopi, Storytellers, l-r: 9.75", 4", 9.25". *Courtesy of Jim Silva.*

Zuni

Kalestewa, Juanita. Zuni, Owl, 1986. *Courtesy of Adobe Gallery.*

Him, Rowina. Zuni, Owl. *Courtesy of Adobe Gallery.*

Tsipa, Sadie. Zuni, Owl. *Courtesy of Adobe Gallery.*

Others
BLACKFOOT

HISPANIC

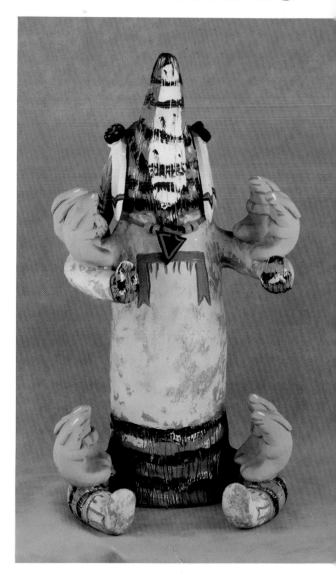

Farrell. Blackfoot, Male storyteller (10 children).
Courtesy of Indian Traders West.

NAVAJO

G.B. Hispanic, Coyote (4 bunnies), 15". *Courtesy of Indian Traders West.*

Atson, Marilyn C. Navajo, Miniatures , 2"-3". *Courtesy of Shiprock Trading Company.*

Atson, Marilyn Clayton. Navajo, Miniatures, 2"-3". *Courtesy of Shiprock Trading Company.*

Atson, Marilyn C. Navajo, Storytellers. *Courtesy of Shiprock Trading Company.*

Atson, Marilyn C. Navajo, Female storyteller (10 children). *Courtesy of Shiprock Trading Company.*

Chacho, L. Navajo, Female, 8". *Courtesy of Bing Crosby's.*

133

Chacho, R. Navajo, Male, 6".
Courtesy of Bing Crosby's.

Chacho, R. Navajo, Females. *Courtesy of Indian Traders West.*

PAPAGO

Kermin, Laura. Papago, Nativity. *Courtesy of Adobe Gallery.*

Creating Storytellers

Joseph and Caroline Gachupin have been making storytellers since 1978 or 1979. Caroline's mother Grace L. Fragua made pots and storytellers. Caroline learned to make figures from her sister, Emily F. Tsosie who made her first cornmaiden in the 1970s. Now her work is recognized as some of the best.

When Joseph began pottery he knew of only one other man doing pottery work. Occasionally he would be teased about doing "women's work," but as he began to be successful the teasing stopped.

They live in the pueblo of Jemez, working in the living room of their home. The people of Jemez are known for their hospitality, and we were the benefactors of this on two occasions when we entered their home to record the process of creating storytellers.

The act of making the storytellers has a spiritual aspect to it. As they are creating them, Joseph and Caroline let the story-tellers know how important they are to the family's livelihood. They talk to the fire, recognizing its power for good and for evil, and ask it to be kind. "He can take everything away from you," said Caroline, "so tell him that we need our income and that we are all depending on him."

Some days Caroline reminds the story-teller she is creating to "sit up straight. You are not going to look good in someone's home looking like that. It's so funny, but it seems like she really does hear you.

"If you are lazy one day, she knows it, and she won't do anything for you. When that happens you just cover her up and put her outside. The next morning you uncover her. 'Maybe today,' you say, and sure enough it works."

As you look at the storytellers, it is easy enough to believe that they have person-alities, that they can hear you, and, certainly, that they have a story to tell.

The pueblo of Jemez and the surrounding hills. Around the village are rich deposits of clay. Each deposit has clay of a different color and quality, and they are used to give the Gachupins' work its color and texture.

Joseph collecting clay. Each potter has their favorite source for clay and is reluctant to share that location with others.

After the clays are prepared, they are used in the traditional coil technique to form the story-tellers. A long strip is rolled in the hands.

Then it is applied to the pot...

Some preliminary preparation of the clay is done at the sight. Later the clay will be ground, and carefully sifted and resifted to remove impurities. Joseph used to sift the clay through panty hose, causing some embarrassment when he went to a store to purchase them. One day he happened upon a sifter in an Asian cookware shop that did the trick. "Thank God I don't have to go in the women's section again!"

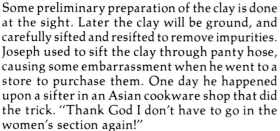

and smoothed.

In this way the pot is gradually built up to the desired size and shape.

A collecting trip may include stops at several spots to obtain the necessary clays.

Joseph is making a cornmaiden storyteller, so he has created a tall slender pot, tapering at the top. The cornmaiden is an important figure in the stories of the Jemez pueblo. Not only is corn a staple part of the Jemez diet, but tribal lore has it that once an ear of corn overheard men conspiring attack the village and was able to sound the warning that saved it.

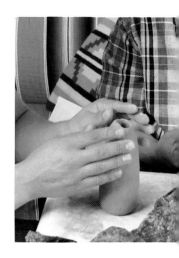

136

When the body portion is shaped, the head is formed separately.

The main features are added to the head...

Then it is placed on the body and the facial features are refined.

Joseph continues the work by rolling long, thin strips of clay...

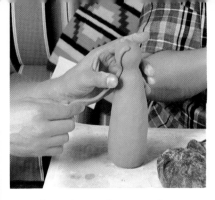

and applying them to the cornmaiden.

The head of the child, who will be peeking out of the cornmaiden's robe, is shaped and given facial features.

After positioning...

A hole is carved in the cornmaiden so that the head may be pegged into her side. This insures that it will be securely attached.

After refining the facial features of the child, Joseph runs the robe of the mother around it and blends the two figures.

Water is used to smooth the surface of the figures. Here Joseph applies it with a brush.

Next, Joseph rolls another strip of clay and cuts it into small segments to be used as kernels of corn.

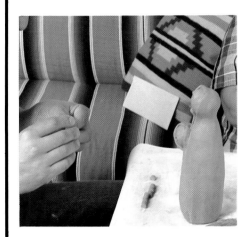

These are then shaped by hand...

and applied in the opening of the cornmaiden's robe, beginning at the top.

The corn pattern will continue down...

making a nice flowing pattern in the opening.

Flat pieces are shaped and applied to the neck area to form a regal cowl.

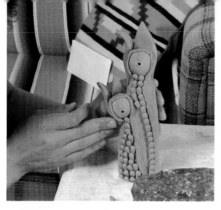

With the cowl added to the child, the cornmaiden nears completion.

Working side-by-side with Joseph and using the same techniques, Caroline creates a sitting storyteller.

After forming the basic shape of the body, Caroline molds the arms...

and applies them to the body.

With moistened fingers she blends them in place.

Next, Caroline forms the head.

After forming the basic facial features...

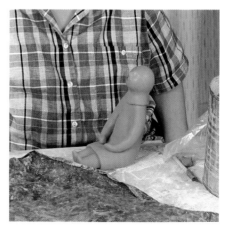

she places the head on the body.

138

Again she moistens her fingers and blends the head with the body.

These lines are smoothed and blended with her fingers.

The children are placed on the mother.

The storyteller thus far.

A bow is added to the back.

A clay peg holds them in place.

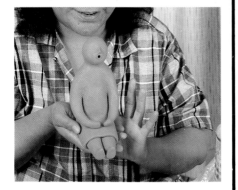

Clay is applied to the head to create the traditional hair style.

The children are formed separately from solid clay.

A moist brush helps smooth the work.

Using a stylus, Caroline marks hairlines in the applied clay.

Facial features are added.

The finished storyteller.

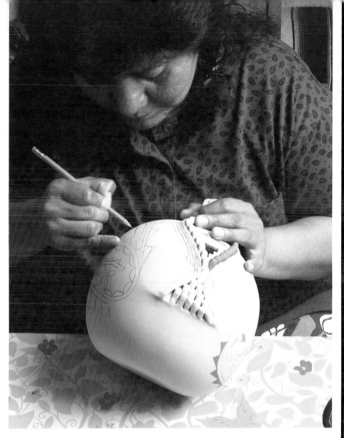

Caroline uses traditional patterns to decorate the story-tellers and other pottery she and Joseph create. After the piece has thoroughly dried she draws the patterns with pencil. This is done freehand, and the pieces vary according to form and Caroline's artistic interpretation.

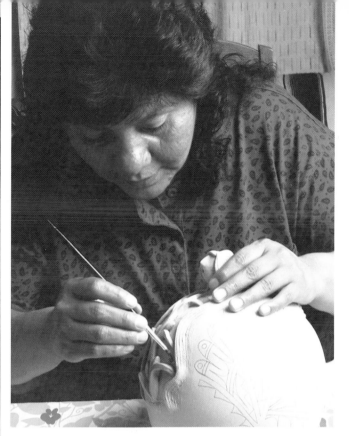

Before painting, the pieces are gone over carefully with a moist brush. This makes the surface smooth. This small brush gets into the little nooks and crannies.

The forms represent clouds, kiva steps, and feathers, as well as other traditional symbols.

A larger brush is used for broader surfaces.

The paints the Gachupins use are made from clay and water, and are applied before firing. This is the traditional way, although some artists use acrylics and other paints, usually applied after firing. They break with tradition by using commercial brushes instead of yucca leaves. Caroline begins with the black paint on the dress. The dress is traditional, coming over one shoulder. It is called a manta.

and the children.

Saving the eyes until the end of the project, Caroline turns to the red clay paint to do the sash...

She continues painting the hair of the mother...

and the mouths of the mother and children.

Next the eyes are painted. Caroline does the eyes for her work and for Joseph's.

Finally Caroline paints the cheeks red...

Using the designs that Caroline has created, Joseph applies the natural paints. First he outlines the pattern, then he fills it in. Four pigments are used: white, gray, black, and red.

Joseph alternates colors, doing one at a time.

bordered with black dots. The red painted cheek used to be a ceremonial custom among Jemez and other pueblo women. Now only the women of Zia pueblo continue the tradition. Caroline's mother, Grace Fragua, used to sign her pieces on the bottom and painted the cheeks red. People used to come and look for her. After her death, Caroline and her sisters and brothers kept the ceremonial trademark. Some others have picked up the cheek painting. When doing a male figure the cheek is painted with a red line, "war paint."